Windows, Rings, and Grapes— a Look at Different Shapes

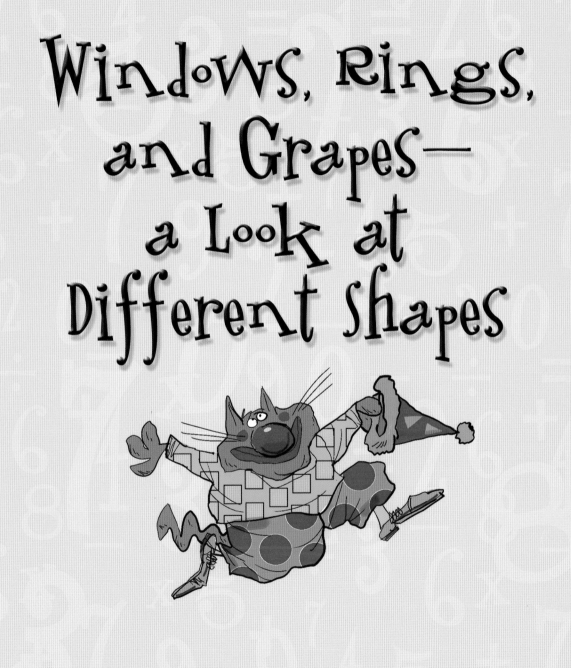

To Ellen
—B.P.C.

Shape:
The form or outline of an object

Windows, Rings, and Grapes— a Look at Different Shapes

by Brian P. Cleary

illustrated by Brian Gable

M MILLBROOK PRESS / MINNEAPOLIS

A shape is a form.
It's how something looks,

with
a top

and a
middle

and bottom.

4

And knowing about them all

inside
and out,

they're easy to name
when you spot 'em.

A circle is round,
like the dot on this gown,

like a Hula-hoop, pie,

or some rings,

PIE
FOR SALE

the door on
this dryer,

a bicycle tire.

The circle forms
all of these things.

7

There's not one straight line
in a circle's design.

It's just a continuous bend.

It's looped and it's curved, and when closely observed, you'll find no beginning or end.

If two dogs would fetch one
and lengthen
and stretch one,

an oval would be

its new shape.

Most racetracks are oval.

If one day you go, you'll
note stretches
that aren't quite as round.

These straightaway places
are perfect for races,
with no curves to make you
slow down.

When three straight lines meet,

the result is quite neat.

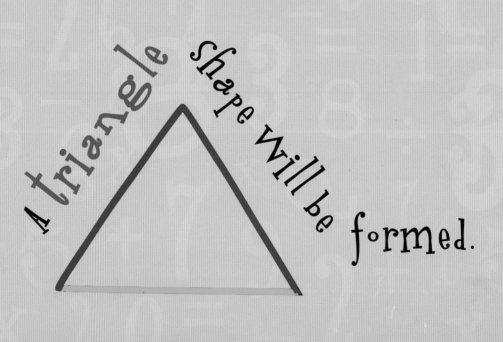

A triangle shape will be formed.

This nice slice of pizza he's trying to heat's a **triangular** treat being warmed.

So, just as a tricycle
has 3 round wheels
and triceratops
has 3 sharp horns,

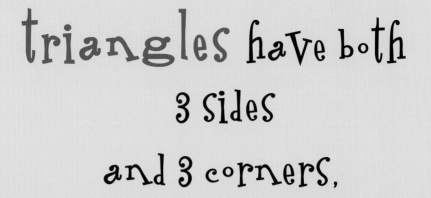

triangles have both
3 sides
and 3 corners,

so try to remember these forms!

The shade your old house had?

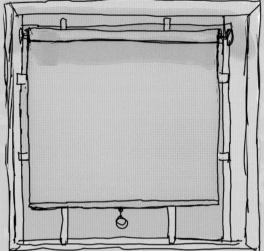

This map?

...or this mouse pad?

Each one of these shapes is a square.

The form is four-sided
and when it's divided,

you'll find four more
squares inside there.

The corners all look

like the edge
of this book—

a bit like an uppercase L.

The sides have to be
all the same length, you see,

like the
windows
in this
new hotel.

23

If two sides were smaller
and the other two taller,

a rectangle is what you'd call it.

It's the shape of this doorway,

this postcard from Norway,

this screen,

and a check and this wallet.

Like a square, only wider,
this billboard for cider
is rectangular
in its shape.

Like a **square**, only taller,
so is this wall or

the frame for this fine
painted ape.

So, When you
see shapes
on the carpet
or drapes,

on your
lunch box
or backpack
or games,

you'll know what to call
every one—big or small—
because you'll know
each of their names!

So, what is a triangle?
What is a rectangle?
What is a square?
What is a circle?
What is an oval?

Do you know?

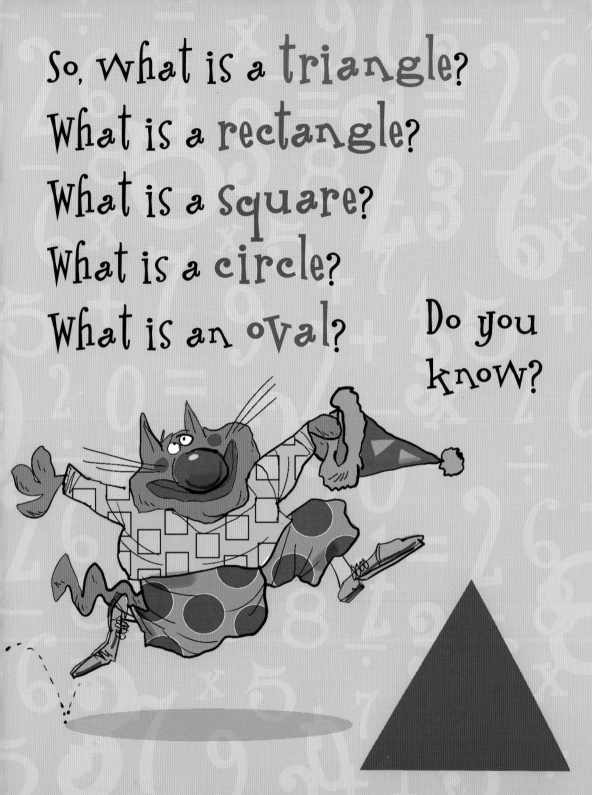

A triangle has three sides and three corners.

A rectangle has four sides and four corners.
The corners are right angles.

A square has four
equal sides and four
corners. The corners
are right angles.

A circle is perfectly round.
It has no corners.

An oval is a shape
like an egg.
It has no corners.

Find activities, games, and more at
www.brianpcleary.com

ABOUT THE AUTHOR & ILLUSTRATOR

BRIAN P. CLEARY is the author of the Words Are Categorical©, Math Is Categorical©, Adventures in Memory™, and Sounds Like Reading™ series. He has also written <u>The Laugh Stand: Adventures in Humor</u>, <u>Peanut Butter and Jellyfishes: A Very Silly Alphabet Book</u>, and two poetry books. Mr. Cleary lives in Cleveland, Ohio.

BRIAN GABLE is the illustrator of many Words Are CATegorical© books, the Math Is CATegorical© series, and the Make Me Laugh! joke books. Mr. Gable also works as a political cartoonist for the <u>Globe and Mail</u> newspaper in Toronto, Canada, where he lives with his children.

Millbrook Press
A division of Lerner Publishing Group, Inc.
241 First Avenue North
Minneapolis, MN 55401 U.S.A.

Website address: www.lernerbooks.com

Library of Congress Cataloging-in-Publication Data

Cleary, Brian P., 1959—
    Windows, rings, and grapes—a look at different shapes / by Brian P. Cleary ; illustrated by Brian Gable.
        p. cm. — (Math is categorical)
    ISBN: 978-0-8225-7879-6 (lib. bdg. : alk. paper)
        1. Shapes—Juvenile literature. I. Gable, Brian, 1949— II. Title.
    QA445.5.C55 2009
    516'.15—dc22   2008044283

Manufactured in the United States of America
1 2 3 4 5 6 — DP — 14 13 12 11 10 09